# BRIGHT SHENG

# MY SONG

## FOR PIANO

T0050920

ED 3904
Revised Printing: May 2019

ISBN: 978-0-7935-3836-2

# G. SCHIRMER, Inc.

DISTRIBUTED BY
HAL•LEONARD®
7777 W. BLUEMOUND RD. P.O. BOX 13819 MILWAUKEE, WI 53213
www.halleonard.com

*to Peter Serkin*

# MY SONG
## I

Bright Sheng

\* Depress keys silently and use sostenuto pedal to sustain the notes until the end of the movement.

\*\* This notation is an attempt to imitate the *glissando* effect of the voice. The duration of the shorter note should
  be played exactly, and the dynamic of the longer note should be slightly louder than the shorter note.

\* Use the finger tip to tap the string inside the piano.
  Make sure to strike the string forcefully so the result sounds "**mp**."

*attacca*

# II

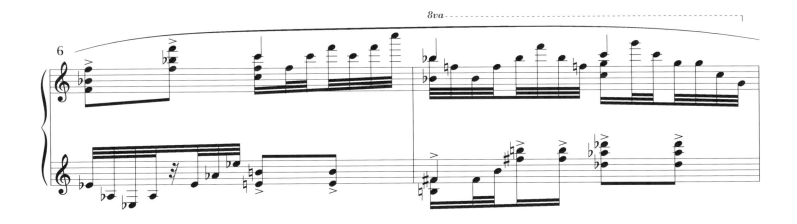

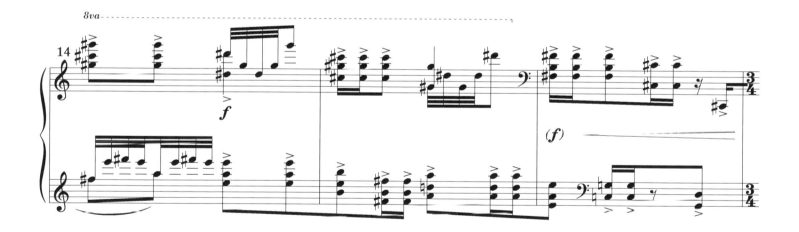

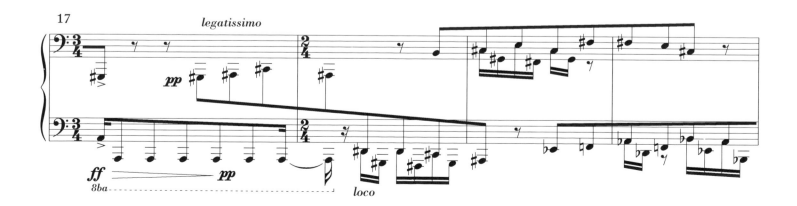

*poco rit.*

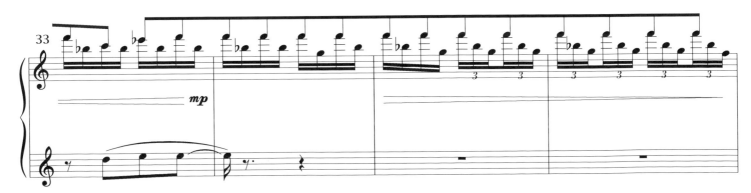

**A tempo**

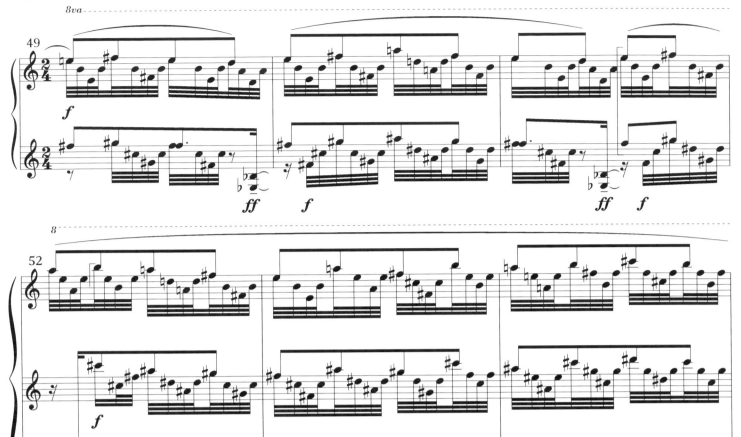

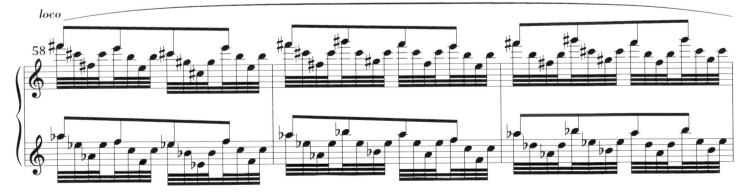

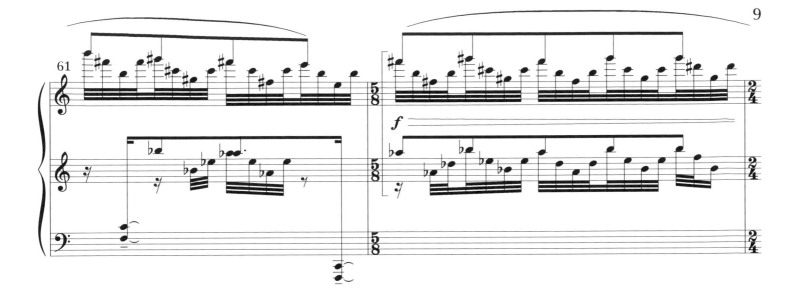

# III

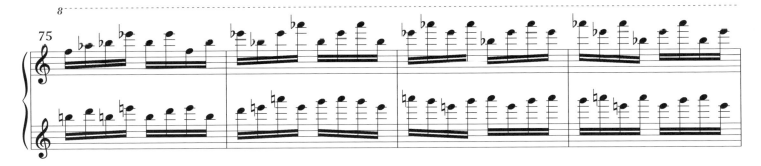

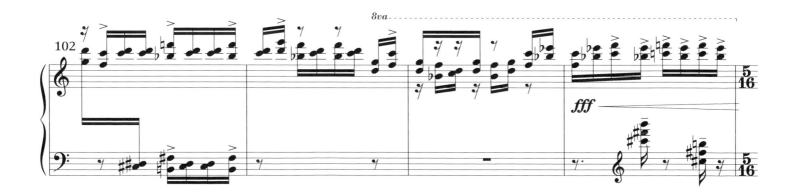

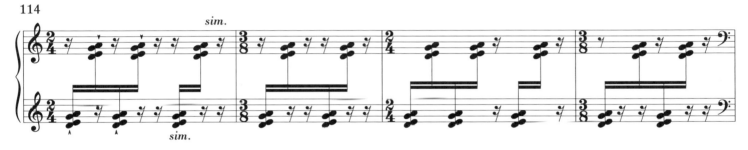

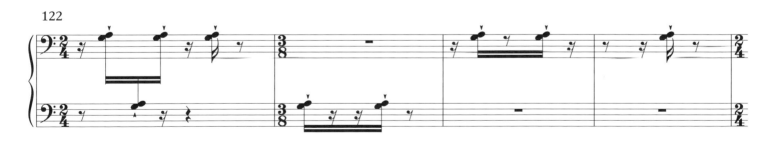

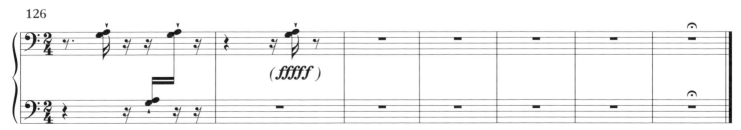

attacca

# IV
## Nostalgia

pp

una corda

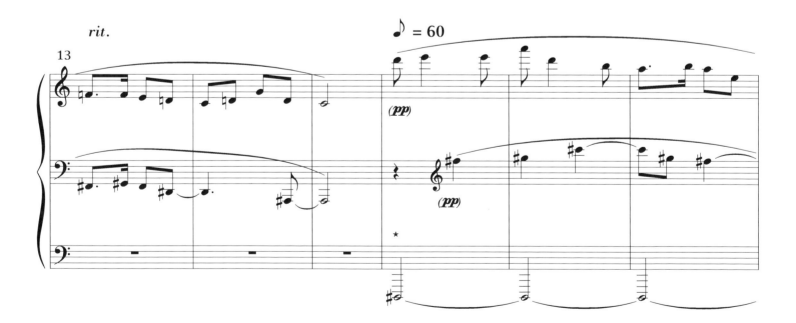

*rit.*

♪ = 60

13

(pp)

(pp)

★

* Both the sustain pedal and the una corda pedal should be pressed down by the left foot here.